LIVE.

BREATH.

WRITE.

USA TODAY Bestselling Author

PEYTON BANKS

ISBN: 978-1-956602-27-2

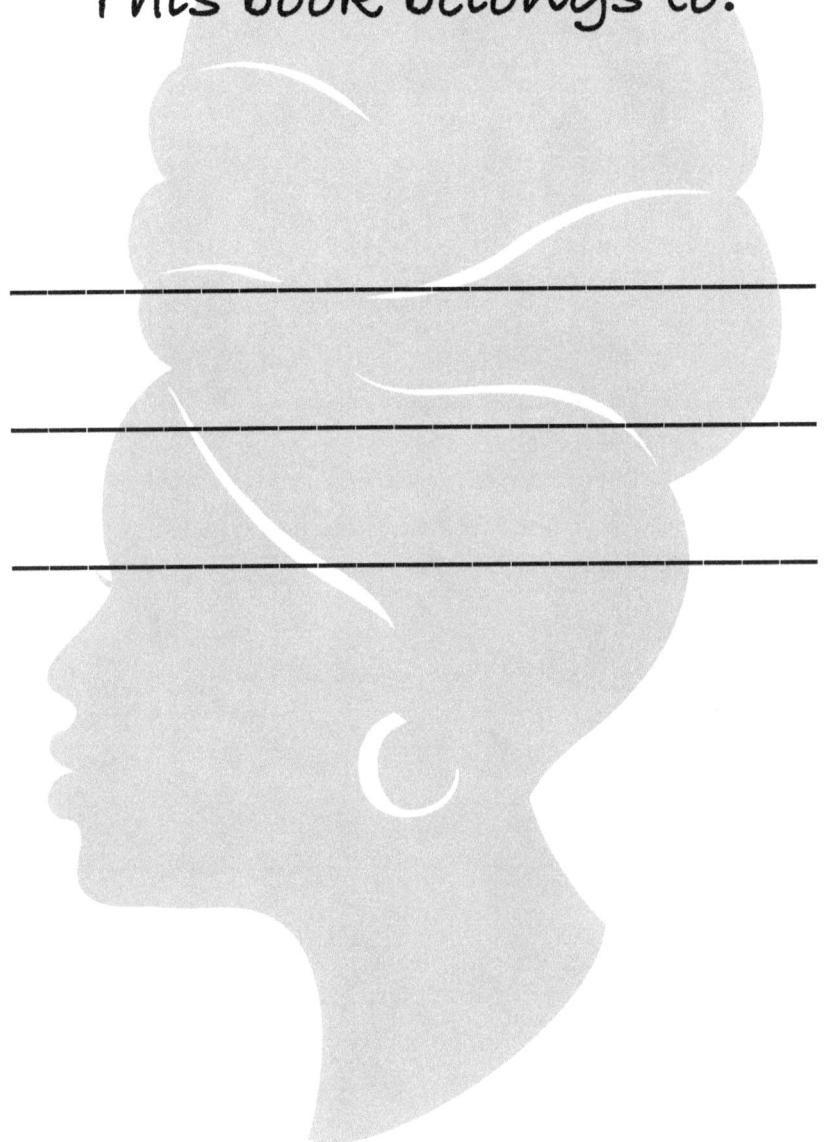

This book belongs to:

_____

_____

_____

"Learn to embrace your own unique beauty, celebrate your unique gifts
with confidence. Your imperfections are actually a gift."
-Kerry Washington